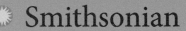 

The Declaration of Independence

Introducing Primary Sources

by Kathryn Clay

CAPSTONE PRESS
a capstone imprint

Little Explorer is published by Capstone Press,
1710 Roe Crest Drive, North Mankato, Minnesota 56003
www.mycapstone.com

Library of Congress Cataloging-in-Publication Data
Names: Clay, Kathryn, author.
Title: Declaration of Independence : introducing primary sources / by Kathryn
    Clay.
Description: North Mankato, Minnesota : Smithsonian Books, Capstone Press,
    2018. | Series: Introducing primary sources | Series: Smithsonian little
    explorer | Includes bibliographical references and index.
Identifiers: LCCN 2017010251
ISBN 9781515763550 (library binding)
ISBN 9781515763604 (paperback)
ISBN 9781515763642 (eBook PDF)
Subjects: LCSH: United States. Declaration of Independence—Juvenile literature. | United
States. Declaration of Independence—Sources—Juvenile literature. | United States—Politics and
government—1775-1783—Juvenile literature.
Classification: LCC E221 .C539 2018 | DDC 973.3/13—dc23
LC record available at https://lccn.loc.gov/2017010251

Editorial Credits
Brenda Haugen, editor; Veronica Scott and Philippa Jenkins, designers;
Kelli Lageson, media researcher; Tori Abraham, production specialist

Our very special thanks to Jim Barber, Historian, National Portrait Gallery, Smithsonian, for his curatorial review. Capstone would also like to thank the following at Smithsonian Enterprises: Kealy Gordon, Product Development Manager, Ellen Nanney, Licensing Manager, Brigid Ferraro, Vice President, Education and Consumer Products, Carol LeBlanc, Senior Vice President, Education and Consumer Products, and Christopher A. Liedel, President.

Photo Credits
We would like to thank the following for permission to reproduce photographs: Alamy: FOR ALAN, 15 (bottom); Bridgeman Images: Peter Newark American Pictures, 15 (top); Compass Point Books: 18; Getty Images: Hulton Archive, 7; Granger, NYC - All rights reserved: 19; iStockphoto: duncan1890, 8; Library of Congress: 4, 5, 6, 13, 16, 25, 27, 28, 29; National Archives and Records Administration: 9, 11; Newscom: akg-images, 12, Reuters/Jonathan Ernst, 26; North Wind Picture Archives: 17; Shutterstock: Joseph Sohm, 10, Sergiy Palamarchuk, 21, StudioOneNine, 20, Susan Law Cain, cover, 23, Timothy R. Nichols, 24, Victorian Traditions, cover (top right)

Table of Contents

Primary Sources...4

First Continental Congress.......................6

A Shot Heard 'Round the World.................8

Second Continental Congress...................10

Committee of Five...................................12

Congress Declares Independence..............14

Sharing the News....................................16

Saving the Declaration...........................18

Parts of the Declaration..........................20

The Body...22

The Declaration and Equal Rights............24

The Declaration of Independence Today.............26

Timeline..28

Glossary..30

Read More...31

Internet Sites..31

Critical Thinking Questions......................32

Index..32

Primary Sources

Primary sources are created during major historical events. They act as evidence of a time or place in history. Paintings, letters, and diaries are all primary sources. People use these things to learn about past events.

An 1818 painting by John Trumbull shows the Declaration of Independence being signed.

The Declaration of Independence is also a primary source. Other primary sources include the U.S. Constitution and the Pledge of Allegiance.

The Declaration of Independence at a Glance

- approved on July 4, 1776

- signed by 56 delegates

- signers include Thomas Jefferson, John Adams, and Benjamin Franklin

- first person to sign was John Hancock

- 200 copies were sent to the American colonies. Only 26 have survived.

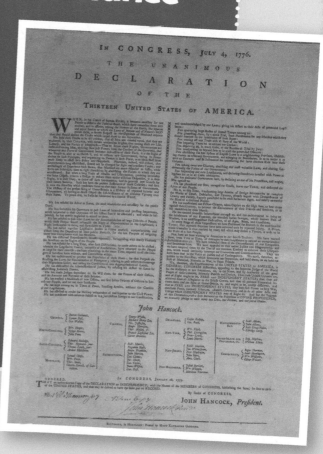

First Continental Congress

The United States was not always its own country. When colonists first came here, the colonies were controlled by Great Britain. Colonists had to follow British laws. They paid expensive taxes for British goods. Some people thought the laws and taxes were unfair. They met in Philadelphia, Pennsylvania, to discuss the laws in September 1774. The group was known as the First Continental Congress.

an engraving of the First Continental Congress by Francois Godefroy

Members of this group did not want to start a war. They did not seek independence. Instead they only hoped to change the laws and lower the taxes. They decided to protest by not buying British goods. They also sent a letter to King George III in Great Britain. The letter explained why colonists were upset. It asked the king to get rid of unfair laws.

NOTHING WAS THOUGHT OF BUT THIS TAXATION, AND THE EASIEST METHOD OF LIQUIDATION.

T-A-X

'TWAS ENOUGH TO VEX THE SOULS OF THE MEN OF BOSTON TOWN, TO READ THIS UNDER THE SEAL OF THE CROWN.

TAX·ON·TEA·
3ᵈ per lb
1773
SALE

THEY WERE LOYAL SUBJECTS OF GEORGE THE THIRD; SO THEY BELIEVED AND SO THEY AVERRED, BUT THIS BRISTLING, OFFENSIVE PLACARD SET ON THE WALLS, WAS WORSE THAN A BAYONET,

a 1767 cartoon showing a colonist learning about the tax on tea

A Shot Heard 'Round the World

King George III did not end the unfair laws. Instead he increased the taxes that colonists were paying for British supplies. Anger grew throughout the colonies. If the king wouldn't listen, colonists were prepared to fight.

The Boston Tea Party

Great Britain spent a lot of money during the French and Indian War (1754–1763). To raise money, Great Britain taxed goods that were sent to the colonies. They taxed sugar, paper, and tea. Colonists did not want to pay the taxes. On December 16, 1773, a group of colonists climbed aboard three British ships docked in Boston Harbor. They dumped chests of tea into the water. This event is now known as the Boston Tea Party.

a vintage engraving of tea being thrown into Boston Harbor

British soldiers marched into Massachusetts looking for weapons on April 18, 1775. They were met by a group of armed patriots. Patriots are people willing to fight for their country. No one knows who fired the first shot. But by the end of the fight, British soldiers had killed eight patriots. Known as the Battles of Lexington and Concord, this marked the start of the American Revolution (1775–1783).

a portrait of the battle at Concord

Second Continental Congress

The war between the colonists and Great Britain continued. In the summer of 1775, the Second Continental Congress met in Philadelphia. Delegates from each colony attended the meetings, including Thomas Jefferson and Benjamin Franklin. Richard Henry Lee of Virginia wanted the colonies to declare independence from Great Britain. But not everyone was ready.

Delegates needed approval from their colonies to vote for independence. The Congress decided to wait three weeks.

Richard Henry Lee's resolution to declare independence June 7, 1776

FACT

The Second Continental Congress created an army to combat the military threat from Britain. It was called the Continental Army.

Committee of Five

The Continental Congress wanted a document prepared in case they voted for independence. They formed a small group of delegates to create this document. The document would explain why America wanted independence. The group was called the Committee of Five.

an 1850 steel engraving based on a painting of the Committee of Five by Alonzo Chappel

COMMITTEE OF FIVE

The Committee of Five was:

Roger Sherman	Connecticut
John Adams	Massachusetts
Benjamin Franklin	Pennsylvania
Thomas Jefferson	Virginia
Robert Livingston	New York

Thomas Jefferson was asked to write out the things the group discussed. He wrote late into the night for more than two weeks. The Committee of Five shared his work with the Continental Congress on June 28, 1776.

Jefferson's rough draft of the Declaration of Independence

FACT

Some of Jefferson's words sounded similar to other works. In the Virginia Declaration of Rights, George Mason wrote that "all men are by nature free and independent and have certain … rights."

Congress Declares Independence

The Continental Congress voted for independence on July 2, 1776. It spent three days looking through Jefferson's draft. Delegates changed words and phrases. In one paragraph Jefferson argued against slavery. Not everyone agreed, so that paragraph was deleted.

The delegates approved the Declaration on July 4, 1776, but the document was not signed until August 2. As president of the Congress, John Hancock was the first to step forward. He signed his name in large letters. Other delegates signed it too. The signed document signaled the end of British rule over the 13 colonies.

a drawing of John Hancock signing the Declaration

FACT

Richard Stockton (left) was a delegate from New Jersey. Stockton was the only signer to take away his support. He was captured by the British and thrown in jail in 1776. After months in jail, he pledged his loyalty to King George III.

Sharing the News

Printed copies of the Declaration of Independence were made the next day. Each of the 13 colonies received copies. General George Washington also received a copy. His troops cheered as the Declaration was read aloud.

an illustration of the first reading of the Declaration printed in *Harper's Weekly* on July 9, 1870

Crowds gathered in large cities to hear the Declaration. People in New York City pulled down a statue of King George III. Others stormed the State House in Boston, Massachusetts. People were excited, but they were also nervous. They knew a long fight was ahead of them.

a hand-colored woodcut of the statue of King George III being pulled down

FACT

The statue of King George III was melted down. The Continental Army used the metal to make more than 42,000 musket balls.

Saving the Declaration

The American Revolution ended in 1783. But by 1814, the United States was at war with Great Britain again. During the War of 1812 (1812–1815), British troops marched toward Washington, D.C. People worried the troops would burn down the War Office Building where the original copy of the Declaration of Independence was kept.

They packed up the important document and moved it to a nearby farm. It was later moved to a house in Leesburg, Virginia. A month later it was brought back to the capital.

FACT

During World War II (1939–1945), the Declaration of Independence was stored at Fort Knox in Kentucky.

a 1991 photograph of Fort Knox

Parts of the Declaration

The Preamble

The Declaration of Independence is made up of three main parts. The first part is called the preamble. It explains why the declaration was written. It is also the most famous part.

Declaration of Independence with feather quill on wood surface

The words of the preamble are often quoted: "We hold these truths to be self-evident, that all men are created equal, that they are endowed by their Creator with certain unalienable Rights, that among these are Life, Liberty and the pursuit of Happiness."

What This Means

"We hold these truths to be self-evident, that all men are created equal, ... "
meaning: these rights do not need to be proved

" ... that they are endowed by their Creator ... "
meaning: God-given rights

" ... with certain unalienable Rights, among these Life, Liberty and the pursuit of Happiness."
meaning: these rights cannot be taken away

the back of a $2 bill showing the painting *The Declaration of Independence* by John Trumbull

The Body

The middle of the declaration includes a list of complaints against King George III. Colonists used these complaints as reasons why they should be their own country.

Some of the complaints included:

"Quartering large bodies of armed troops among us ... "
meaning: colonists were forced to feed and house British troops

" ... imposing Taxes without our Consent ... "
meaning: colonists had to pay taxes that they didn't approve of

" ... plundered our seas, ravaged our Coasts, burnt our towns, and destroyed the lives of our people."
meaning: King George III declared war on the colonists

The Final Section

The last paragraph states the colonies are now free from Britain's rule. The name United States of America is first used here. At the bottom are the signatures of 56 of the 58 delegates.

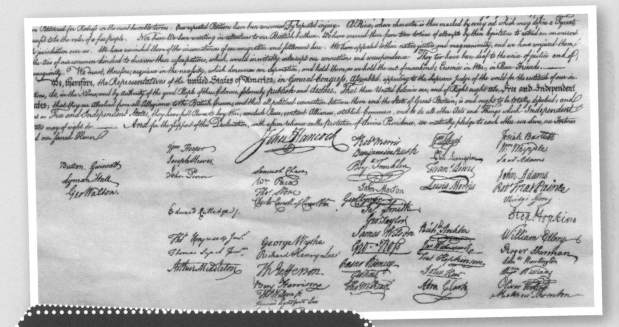

FACT

Delegates John Dickinson and Robert R. Livingston did not sign the Declaration of Independence.

The Declaration and Equal Rights

In his famous Gettysburg Address speech, President Abraham Lincoln used language from the Declaration of Independence. He said, "All men are created equal."

a reproduction of the Gettysburg Address

Civil rights leader Martin Luther King Jr. also used these words. In his I Have a Dream speech, King argued that these words meant that people of all races should be treated the same.

a photo showing the crowd gathered for Lincoln's speech

Lincoln

The Declaration of Independence Today

The original Declaration of Independence is located in Washington, D.C.

Visitors to the National Archives in Washington, D.C., view the Declaration of Independence, preserved under glass and special lighting, on July 3, 2013.

Both the Declaration and the original U.S. Constitution are displayed in the Rotunda for the Charters of Freedom. The Rotunda is located in the National Archives Museum. The document is protected by a titanium case and bulletproof glass. At night it is put in a safe made of steel and concrete. The parchment was rolled and unrolled many times. Over the years the document has faded. But the words remain as important as ever.

FACT

For years people wondered about a word that was smudged on the Declaration. Recently high-tech instruments using infrared and ultraviolet light were able to solve the mystery. Instead of using the word "citizens," Jefferson first used the word "subjects." He changed the word because people of the United States were not to be ruled as they were in Great Britain.

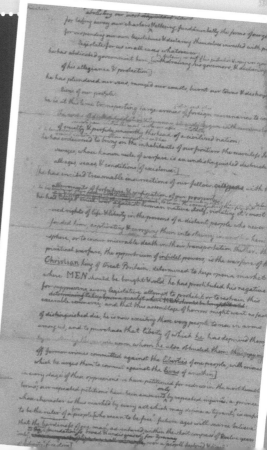

Timeline

an illustration on a 1903 postcard of the burning of the Stamp Act in Boston

1765   Great Britain's Stamp Act puts a tax on all paper documents in the American colonies

1770   British soldiers fire on a crowd, killing five colonists during the Boston Massacre

1773   The Sons of Liberty dump 342 chests of tea into Boston Harbor to protest high taxes on tea during the Boston Tea Party

1774   The First Continental Congress meets in Philadelphia

1775   Shot heard 'round the world at the Battles of Lexington and Concord. American Revolution begins.

June 7, 1776   Richard Henry Lee urges Congress to declare independence from Great Britain

June 11, 1776   Committee of Five is appointed to draft the Declaration of Independence

June 12–27, 1776	Jefferson writes a draft of the Declaration of Independence
July 1–4, 1776	Continental Congress debates and revises the Declaration of Independence
July 2, 1776	Continental Congress declares independence
July 4, 1776	Continental Congress adopts the Declaration of Independence
August 2, 1776	Delegates begin signing the Declaration of Independence
1777	Signed copies are sent to the states
1783	American Revolution ends
1863	President Abraham Lincoln gives his Gettysburg Address speech
1952	Declaration of Independence is moved to the National Archives
1963	Martin Luther King Jr. gives his I Have a Dream speech

the hall of the National Archives building in Washington, D.C., where the Declaration of Independence is displayed

Glossary

colonist—someone who lives in a newly settled area

Continental Congress—leaders from the 13 original American colonies who made up the American government from 1774 to 1789

convention—a formal meeting

declaration—a public announcement

delegate—a person chosen to represent a larger group of people at a meeting

evidence—information and facts that help prove something or make you believe that something is true or false

independence—freedom from the control of others

musket ball—a ball made of lead that is shot from a gun with a long barrel

parchment—a paper-like substance for writing on, usually made of animal skin

Patriot—a colonist loyal to America during the American Revolution

primary source—an original document

protest—to object to something strongly and publicly

quote—to repeat or copy

revolt—to rise up or fight back against a government or an authority

slavery—the owning of another person; slaves are forced to work without pay

tax—money that people or businesses must pay to the government

Read More

Ferguson, Melissa. *American Symbols: What You Need to Know?* Fact Files. North Mankato, Minn: Capstone Press, 2017.

Manger, Katherine. T*he Declaration of Independence.* Let's Find Out! Primary Sources. New York: Rosen Education Services, 2017.

Miller, Mirella S. *12 Questions About the Declaration of Independence.* Examining Primary Sources. Mankato, Minn.: 12-Story Library, 2016.

Shamir, Ruby. *What's the Big Deal About Freedom?* New York: Philomel Books, 2017.

Internet Sites

Use FactHound to find Internet sites related to this book.

Visit www.facthound.com

Just type in 9781515763550 and go.

Check out projects, games and lots more at
www.capstonekids.com

Critical Thinking Questions

1. A declaration is a public statement. Give an example of a public statement you have heard recently on the news or at school.

2. What were the reasons the American colonists declared independence from Great Britain? Use the text to help you with your answer.

3. The Declaration of Independence is made up of three parts. What are those three parts?

Index

Adams, John, 5, 12

American Revolution, 9, 18

Battles of Lexington and Concord, 9

Boston Tea Party, 8

Committee of Five, 12, 13

First Continental Congress, 6–7

Franklin. Benjamin, 5, 10, 12

French and Indian War, 8

George III, King, 7, 8, 15, 17, 22

Hancock, John, 5, 14

Jefferson, Thomas, 5, 10, 12, 13, 14, 27

Lee, Richard Henry, 10

parts of the Declaration, 20–23

Pledge of Allegiance, 5

primary sources, 4

Second Continental Congress, 10–14

taxes, 6, 7, 8, 22

U.S. Constitution, 5, 27

War of 1812, 18